# Conversat__
### for

### Jonas Jonasson's

# The 100-Year-Old Man Who Climbed Out the Window and Disappeared

## BydailyBooks

**FREE Download: Get the Hottest Books!**
*Get Your Free Books with **<u>Any Purchase</u>** of Conversation Starters!*

 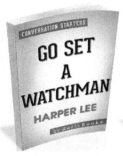 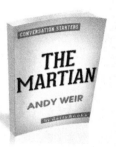

Every purchase comes with a FREE download of the hottest titles!

*Add spice to any conversation*
*Never run out of things to say*
*Spend time with those you love*

**Read it for FREE on any smartphone, tablet, Kindle, PC or Mac.**
No purchase necessary - licensed for personal enjoyment only.

**Get it Now**

or Click Here.

**Scan Your Phone**

**Please Note: This is an unofficial Conversation Starters guide. If you have not yet read the original work, please do so first.**

**Copyright © 2015 by dailyBooks. All Rights Reserved.
First Published in the United States of America 2015**

*We hope you enjoy this complementary guide from* **Read2Lead.** *We aim to provide quality, thought provoking material to assist in your discovery and discussions on some of today's favorite books.*

Disclaimer / Terms of Use: Product names, logos, brands, and other trademarks featured or referred to within this publication are the property of their respective trademark holders and are not affiliated with Read2Lead. The publisher and author make no representations or warranties with respect to the accuracy or completeness of these contents and disclaim all warranties such as warranties of fitness for a particular purpose. This guide is unofficial and unauthorized. It is not authorized, approved, licensed, or endorsed by the original book's author or publisher and any of their licensees or affiliates.

No part of this publication may be reproduced or retransmitted, electronic or mechanical, without the written permission of the publisher.

**Tips for Using Read2Lead Conversation Starters:**

EVERY GOOD BOOK CONTAINS A WORLD FAR DEEPER THAN the surface of its pages. The characters and their world come alive through the words on the pages, yet the characters and its world still live on. Questions herein are designed to bring us beneath the surface of the page and invite us into the world that lives on. These questions can be used to:

- Foster a deeper understanding of the book
- Promote an atmosphere of discussion for groups
- Assist in the study of the book, either individually or corporately
- Explore unseen realms of the book as never seen before

**About Us:**

THROUGH YEARS OF EXPERIENCE AND FIELD EXPERTISE, from newspaper featured book clubs to local library chapters, *Read2Lead* can bring your book discussion to life. Host your book party as we discuss some of today's most widely read books.

**Table of Contents**

Introducing *The 100-Year-Old Man Who Climbed Out the Window and Disappeared*
Introducing the Author

question 1
question 2
question 3
question 4
question 5
question 6
question 7
question 8
question 9
question 10
question 11
question12
question 13
question 14
question 15
question 16
question 17
question 18
question 19
question 20
question21
question22
question 23
question 24
question 25
question 26
question 27
question 28
question 29
question 30
question 31

- [question 32](#)
- [question 33](#)
- [question 34](#)
- [question 35](#)
- [question 36](#)
- [question 37](#)
- [question 38](#)
- [question 39](#)
- [question 40](#)
- [question 41](#)
- [question 42](#)
- [question 43](#)
- [question 44](#)
- [question 45](#)
- [question 46](#)
- [question 47](#)
- [question 48](#)
- [question 49](#)
- [question 50](#)

# Introducing *The 100-Year-Old Man Who Climbed Out the Window and Disappeared*

*THE 100-YEAR-OLD MAN WHO CLIMBED OUT THE WINDOW AND Disappeared* alternates between the past and the present. Presently, the main character finds himself escaping the nursing home in which he finds himself "trapped," and the past represents the last 100 years of his life in which he experienced many significant events in history.

Allan Karlsson believes he is "trapped" in this nursing home and is, quite frankly, tired of being told what to do, and more importantly, how much vodka he can drink. He is in good health and does not think he belongs in the home. So, one day, as his friends are getting ready for his 100th birthday party, he decides to run away. On his way toward freedom, Karlsson accidentally finds himself in the possession of another man's suitcase. The man had asked him to watch it for him as he waited for the bus, and when the bus arrived, Karlsson could wait no longer and took the suitcase with him.

Karlsson carries the suitcase with him while on his adventure, which comes to represent the "baggage" that he has been carrying for years. He meets many "friends" along the way, including an elephant with whom he is able to share his life story allowing him to unload some of the baggage he has carried all these years. In a *Forest Gump*-style prose, the book takes us through the past 100 years of Allan's life. As an expert in explosives, Allan has met many important people over the years, including Francisco Franco, Harry Truman, Richard Nixon, Winston Churchill, Joseph Stalin, and more. In a humorous twist, we come to find out that Karlsson himself invented the atomic bomb, by accident.

Unbeknownst to him, the suitcase he is carrying throughout this adventure is filled with very important contents. He ends up with criminals and law enforcement chasing after him; however, he always seems to be one step ahead of them. This chase makes for a very humorous story as the readers follow the blundering authorities and criminals who are unable catch up to this 100-year-old man. The reader will have to decide if Allan Karlsson is a mastermind or just an elderly man who stumbles upon the happenings of the story.

# Introducing the Author

JONAS JONASSON IS THE YOUNGEST OF THREE BROTHERS. HE WAS BORN in a town in the south of Sweden called Växjö. Jonasson has been in love with writing since he was a child. After studying Swedish and Spanish in college, he took a job at Sweden's largest newspaper, *Expressen*. He was very successful and was destined to become a key player at *Expresson* when he made the decision to quit the newspaper game in 1994. He then became a media consultant, and later turned to television and became a TV producer.

Although he was very busy with his media company, he was able to find the time to write, little-by-little, what would eventually become his debut novel, *The Hundred-Year-Old Man Who Climbed Out the Window and Disappeared*. Jonasson says that writing helped him deal with the stress of running a successful media company. In 2003, Jonasson sold his media empire and moved to a remote part of Sweden because of his poor health.

Jonasson moved to Switzerland to be with his first wife and their son. Unfortunately, their relationship was in trouble, and they would eventually divorce. While he was in Switzerland, he began writing with the goal of getting his novel published. He used writing to escape the negativity he was experiencing living with his then wife. Jonasson was granted sole custody of his son and he decided to move back to Sweden.

He finished his first novel while living in Sweden. He was rejected by five of six Swedish publishers. Jonasson had imagined having a book deal in his twenties, although he is happy he waited. After such a long wait, he believes he found his own voice rather than imitating the voices of his favorite writers. Unfortunately, the initial success of the novel coincided with the breakup of his marriage, so he was unable to enjoy the success at first.

# *Discussion Questions*

### question 1

When Allan Karlsson first left the nursing home, he went to a bus stop where a man asked him to watch his suitcase. Karlsson decided to take the suitcase with him when the bus arrived. Do you think Karlsson's trip would have been different if he had known the significance of the suitcase when he took it with him? What do you think he would have done differently if he had known?

## question 2

When Allan Karlsson was six years old, his father got into trouble for being outspoken about his social beliefs. He was considered an angry man to everyone except his family. In what ways do you think the character of Allan's father influenced Allan's character?

## question 3

Allan Karlsson was an explosives expert, which brought him into contact with many important historical figures over the years. How do you think the interactions with the historical figures would have been different if he had had a different career?

## question 4

The character of Allan Karlsson is optimistic and has a funny personality. How does Allan's personality affect the story? In what way do you think the story would be different if Allan's personality were different?

## question 5

As a rule, our society expects older people to act a certain way. Do you think Allan's character reflected society's expectations of an older gentleman? In what ways did he meet expectations? In what ways did he challenge expectations?

## question 6

This book included several events relating to real history. Do you think the events were mostly historically accurate? Tell why or why not.

## question 7

The storyline seemed to include some political ideals throughout. What political worldview do you think the author holds? List examples from the story that support this worldview.

## question 8

The main character, Allan Karlsson, is 100 years old. How does his age affect the story? Do you think the book would have been better or worse with a younger protagonist? Why or Why not?

## question 9

Allan Karlsson's final straw in his decision to escape the nursing home is the party his friends are throwing to celebrate his 100${}^{th}$ birthday. What do you think he was escaping when he climbed out the window? Tell about a time when you considered climbing out a window to escape a situation.

### question 10

In most books today, the star of the story is younger. Do you think younger people will see Allan Karlsson as a role model despite his age? Why or Why not?

### question 11

Allan reveals his past through stories. While you were reading the novel, did it occur to you that the stories may have been made up or did you trust Allan? Explain your feelings and what may have contributed to them.

. . . . . . . . . . . . . . . . . . . . . . . . . . . .

### question 12

A satire is a literary work that uses wit, sarcasm, or ridicule. Do you think this book is a satire? If so, what is the subject of the satirization?

. . . . . . . . . . . . . . . . . . . . . . . . . . . .

### question 13

Allan Karlsson does not seem to think his life experiences are important. As you read the story, though, you see the significance of some of his experiences. Why do you think Allan has a different perspective?

### question 14

The end of the book seems to leave room for more. Do you think the author will write a sequel? Would you read a sequel? Why or why not?

## question 15

At the bus station after Karlsson escapes, he buys a ticket to "nowhere." What do you think the author meant by "nowhere"? Tell about a time in your life when you were ready to buy a ticket to nowhere.

### question 16

In a 2013 review, *Novelicious* said the book seemed like a group of short stories that were stitched together to make an effortless read. Do you agree with the reviewer? Is this a positive element of the book or do you think it negatively affected the flow of the story?

## question 17

Of the many historical figures considered for the book, the author chose not to include Adolf Hitler because he did not want to turn the Holocaust into a satire. Do you agree with this decision? Why or why not?

### question 18

A reviewer from *Publisher's Weekly* commented about how the way Jonasson weaves Stalin, Einstein, and Truman into this story makes readers "laugh out loud." Do agree with this opinion? Why or why not?

## question 19

Some readers compare Allan Karlsson's view on life to Forest Gump in the popular movie. He is quoted as saying, 'Whatever happens, happens.' Do you subscribe to this view in your own life? Why or why not?

## question 20

One reviewer said that Allan Karlsson is able to find action and adventure seemingly wherever he goes. Do you agree with this statement? How do you think this tendency added to the story?

**FREE Download: Get the Hottest Books!**
*Get Your Free Books with **Any Purchase** of* Conversation Starters!

  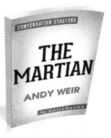

Every purchase comes with a FREE download of the hottest titles!

*Add spice to any conversation*
*Never run out of things to say*
*Spend time with those you love*

**Read it for FREE on any smartphone, tablet, Kindle, PC or Mac.**
No purchase necessary - licensed for personal enjoyment only.

Get it Now

or Click Here.

**Scan Your Phone**

**question 21**

The author himself described the book as "an intelligent, very stupid novel."
Why do you think he said this about his book?

## question 22

One reviewer said that Jonasson's writing of the story was "amusingly deadpan." What do you think the reviewer meant by this and how do you think this style of writing affected the story?

## question 23

One reviewer wrote that the main character is a shameless, unpredictable, foolish, alcoholic man who is unable to see how his actions affect people on a larger scale. They went on to say how the novel is not "feel-good" as the author suggests, rather, it is an absurd and silly story that leaves the reader "half-shocked" and laughing as they would at an "inappropriate, but very funny, joke." Do you agree with this reviewer about the appropriateness of the author's humor? Do you think this type of humor is becoming more accepted in society today?

## question 24

One reviewer said that the main themes of this novel were "coincidence and absurdity." Do you think these were positive elements for this particular story? Why or why not?

## question 25

The *Sunday Times* called the story "loopily freewheeling" and scathingly humorous about a man who is aging "disgracefully." Do you agree with this review? Is Allan aging "disgracefully"?

## question 26

In an attempt to create a new life for himself, Jonas Jonasson sold everything he owned and left behind his journalism and consulting careers. He then took off for Switzerland to be with his wife and son. Life did not work out for him in Switzerland, however. Despite the struggles he had in Switzerland, do you think this was a good life decision for Jonasson? Would you have made the same decision? Why or why not?

## question 27

Jonasson is known for changing the way the world sees Swedish writers. Compare Jonasson's writing to that of Stieg Larsson, who wrote *The Girl with the Dragon Tattoo* series.

## question 28

Jonasson was in the midst of a failing marriage as he was writing his debut novel. In what ways do you think such an event might have affected his writing process?

## question 29

Jonasson has said that he had planned to be a published author in his twenties; however, his first book wasn't published until his late forties. Do you think a 20 plus year age difference would make a difference in his writing? In what ways do you think his writing style would have been different if he had chosen writing as a career earlier in his life?

## question 30

After college, Jonasson became a journalist and later owned a media company. He has said that his media company added a great deal of stress in his life. In what ways do think this high-stress lifestyle contributed to or hindered his writing?

## question 31

In the book, Allan felt so trapped in his nursing home that he ran away. How would you feel if you were in this situation? Would you run away?

## question 32

If you were waiting for a bus at the station and a stranger asked you to watch a bag for him, would you? Why or why not? Would you be curious and open the bag or take the bag with you? What kind of contents would you hope were in the bag?

### question 33

The main character in the book was 100 years old. In what ways would the story have been different if Karlsson was younger?

## question 34

Karlsson always seemed to be one step ahead of everyone chasing him. If you were chasing him, what strategies would you have used to help catch up to this seemingly impossible-to-catch old man?

. . . . . . . . . . . . . . . . . . . . . . . . . .

### question 35

In what ways would Allan Karlsson's story have been different if he had attended the party and just shared his life experience with his friends and family instead of random people?
. . . . . . . . . . . . . . . . . . . . . . . . . .

## question 36

Allan Karlsson bought a ticket to "nowhere." If you were running away, where would your ticket take you and why?

## question 37

Jonasson met his wife on an online dating site. Would you ever consider using an online dating site? Why or why not?

## question 38

Author Jonas Jonasson was not able to fully enjoy the success of his first novel because he was in the midst of a divorce. Would you have held off on the release of the novel so that you could fully enjoy the success? Why or why not?

## *Quiz Questions*

### question 39

**True or False:** *The Hundred-Year-Old Man Who Climbed Out the Window and Disappeared* is about a young man who escapes his day care center and goes on a fun adventure throughout his neighborhood.

### question 40

_____ was used to represent Allan Karlsson's emotional baggage.

**question 41**

The novel is often compared to the movie_____.

**question 42**

Allan Karlsson was an expert in _____.

## question 43

**True or False:** Karlsson meets a giraffe on his adventure.

## question 44

**True or False:** Allan Karlsson is excited about his upcoming birthday celebration.

### question 45

**True or False:** Allan Karlsson meets Albert Einstein's brother in the story.

## question 46

**True or False:** Jonas Jonasson was the youngest of three brothers.

**question 47**

Jonas Jonasson was born in _____.

**question 48**

Jonas Jonasson's debut novel was _____.

## question 49

**True or False:** Jonasson now lives in Switzerland with his wife and child.

## question 50

**True or False:** Jonasson sold his media company partly because of poor health.

## *QuizAnswers*

1. False; it is about an elderly man who escapes his nursing home
2. A suitcase
3. Forrest Gump by Winston Groom
4. Explosives
5. False; he meets an elephant
6. False; he is dreading the party
7. True
8. True
9. Sweden
10. *The Hundred-Year-Old Man Who Climbed Out of a Window and Disappeared*
11. False; Jonasson and his wife are now divorced
12. True

## THE END

## Want to promote your book group? Register here.

PLEASE LEAVE US A FEEDBACK.

*THANK YOU!*

**FREE Download: Get the Hottest Books!**
*Get Your Free Books with **Any Purchase** of* Conversation Starters!

 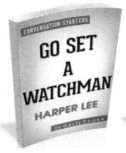 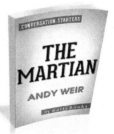

Every purchase comes with a FREE download of the hottest titles!

*Add spice to any conversation*
*Never run out of things to say*
*Spend time with those you love*

**Read it for FREE on any smartphone, tablet, Kindle, PC or Mac.**
No purchase necessary - licensed for personal enjoyment only.

**Get It Now**

or Click Here.

**Scan Your Phone**

Printed in Great Britain
by Amazon